Bless and Curse Not!

Also by Dr. Gwynn

Easter-Not What You Think

Chrislam – What Communion Hath Light
With Darkness?

Conflict – Christianity's Love vs. Islam's
Submission

The President Was a Good Man

Anything for Acceptance

Healing – The Children's Bread

Created to Live!

The gods Among Us

Bless and Curse Not!

Dr. Murl Edward Gwynn

Published by MEG Enterprises Publications
PO Box 2165
Reidsville, GA 30453
(912) 557-6507
meg@kencable.net
www.murlgwynn.com

Unless otherwise identified, Scripture quotations
are from the Holy Bible New International
Version, copyright © 1973, 1978, 1984 by
International Bible Society. Zondervan Publishing
House. Used by permission.

Scripture quotations marked KJV are from the
King James Version of the Bible.

ISBN: 978-0-9711766-4-5

Printed in the U.S.A

TABLE OF CONTENTS

ACKNOWLEDGMENTS

Ruth, my best friend and only wife!

PREFACE

Blessing and cursing is in the power of our tongues and the belief system we adhere to. God wants to bless us in all realms of our lives. There is nothing He leaves out in wanting to bless us and He goes to great lengths to prove just that.

It is sad, however, that so many people totally ignore or deny God's input into our lives and refuse to acknowledge His sovereignty. Because of this we miss out on God's blessings and end up realizing the results of the curse.

We must first know that God does not want to curse and in all reality He does not curse, but just does not bless. When we do see in scripture that God is cursing someone or nation it is in all reality their own doing that forced God to not bless. There are very few scripture references that show God activity cursing someone.

Even when Adam and Eve sinned the earth was cursed not by God but by Adam and His listening to the serpent instead of God; thereby turning the rule ship of the earth over to the enemy of his soul. Once the enemy was in control the earth became corrupt and would not produce as God intended. The curse was Adam's doing and not God's!

It never ceases to amaze me how far we have gotten away from a once firm conviction to never compromise when it comes to God's word and obedience to it.

Holy Scripture, from the Old Testament and all through the New Testament, warns God's children of deviating from His will and commands. God's warnings are not to keep a people in line with a dictatorial ruler or stern potentate, but to insure that the objects of His love remain pure, healthy, and fit in a corrupt and sin infested world. Mankind is the object of God's love!

God warns us to not worship false gods or to align ourselves with anything that comes from

Satan or other dark and contrary beings. God goes as far as to say that He will hold every person accountable for their beliefs, actions, and thoughts, even in ignorance. In other words, our ignorance is no excuse once we are informed of truth.

Many Christians, in solid believing churches, observe the resurrection of Jesus, call it Easter, and celebrate it with eggs, bunnies, and the trappings associated with Easter. Most know that even the word Easter is the modern name for Astrate, a false goddess, which in ancient times was worshipped using sexual and fertility rites. It doesn't seem to matter that we shouldn't have anything to do with even mentioning the name Easter. Some even acknowledge that they know it is wrong, but still practice the egg hunts, bunnies, and bunny cakes. I am amazed! God won't bless in this environment.

Also, many Christians, dabble with items such as horoscopes, numerology, figurines, good luck charms, and other items that are associated with powers of darkness. In most cases, however, I believe they do it in ignorance. Because of the association with powers of darkness, whether in ignorance or not, many believers are sick in body, soul, and spirit. When we do these things we open up our lives to demons and workings of darkness.

I must add here, by no means am I blaming, judging, or condemning anyone. I am, however, trying to help the Church realize a truth that I think will free us in many areas if we will respond according to the will of God.

It is my desire that the information in this book will help us cast off those things that are against God's will and often pull us down and away from the best God has for us.

I believe we bind God's hands from bringing the best (blessings) to us, which is His desire. I believe in our ignorance we fail to realize the best (blessings), when in reality we only realize portion. God wants to give us the maximum but can't, and we scrape to receive minimum.

It is my desire to help you, reader, to cast off all those things that keep you from realizing God's best (blessings). If we will truly obey God and His word, without compromising anything, I am convinced we will be the glorious Church He intended us to be.

1

Belief

Romans 12:14 Bless those who persecute you; bless and do not curse.

Proverbs 26:2 As the bird by wandering, as the swallow by flying, so the curse causeless shall not come.

Matthew 5:44 But I say unto you, Love your enemies, bless them that curse you, do good to them that hate you,

and pray for them which despitefully use you, and persecute you

Galatians 3:13 Christ hath redeemed us from the curse of the law, being made a curse for us: for it is written, Cursed is every one that hangeth on a tree: 14 That the blessing of Abraham might come on the Gentiles through Jesus Christ; that we might receive the promise of the Spirit through faith.

It makes all the difference in the world what comes into and what we permit in our lives. We permit everything into our lives either by omission or commission. Omission[1] can either be an understood omitting of truth, refusing to respond to understood directions, or out-right rebellion to truth. Commission[2] is

---

[1] Omission = 1:something neglected or left undone, 2: the act of omitting : the state of being omitted.

[2] Commission = 1 : a warrant granting certain powers and imposing certain duties 2 : a certificate conferring military rank and authority 3 : authority to act as agent for another; also : something to be done by an agent 4 : a body of persons charged

2

the willful consent, acted upon, either in word or deed, which brings about a desired result. When it comes to God's word and obedience, omission can result in spiritual darkness, death, or disease. On the other hand, if we purposely commission ourselves to obey God and His word we will realize the results that He intended for His children. Those results would always be good!

It is very important that we examine what we believe and then follow through with those beliefs to God's desired result. Often we confess that we know or believe certain things from God's word, but we fail to carry through to completion.

---

with performing a duty 5 : the doing of some act; also : the thing done 6 : the allowance made to an agent for transacting business for another

In Finis Dake's book *Power over Sickness and Disease*[3], Dake shares the following:

> In Isaiah 45:7 we read, "I create evil." The Hebrew word for "evil" is *ra*, meaning "adversity," "affliction," "calamity," "grief," "misery," "sorrow," "wretchedness," "trouble," "harm," "distress," "ill," and "mischief." These things are the harvest of sowing and breaking the laws of God. This is a law fixed by God, and it cannot be altered or changed. **If any free moral agent chooses to break laws, contrary to his creative makeup and the highest good of his being and of the universe, he must pay the penalty of reaping what he has sown**.
>
> When the Bible says that God puts physical sickness and disease upon men, as in the following Scriptures, it simply means that His law of sowing and reaping is being executed by the proper agencies to enforce this law (Exod. 15:26; Deut. 7:15; 28:1-68). In these passages it is stated that sickness is the result of sowing

---

[3] http://yourlastresort.net/index.cfm?PageID=5713

sin. If there had been no sin there would have been no disease. In many places where it speaks of God taking a certain action, in reality He used proper agents actually to bring it to pass. It is said that God sent Joseph into Egypt, but in reality his brethren were the ones who sold him to the Ishmaelites (Gen. 45:4-8). It is said that God would visit Israel and lead them out of Egypt, but in reality God used Moses and Aaron as his agents to do this (Gen. 50:24; Ps. 77:20). It is said on numerous occasions that God subdued Israel's enemies, but in reality He used human agency to do it (Judg. 4:14-23). The same is true of the law of sickness and disease. He has given the actual power of this law into the hands of demon powers.

MAN THE LAW-BREAKER. Man is the great law-breaker, and he must reap what he sows. Man is responsible in the first place for yielding to sin and Satan and submitting to demon powers that take advantage of his sinful state and cause all kinds of failures and sufferings in his life. He is responsible for breaking God's laws; for living in lusts and uncleanness, which breeds sickness and disease; for accidents due to careless living; for lack of *power from God to defeat Satan; for lack of proper exercise; for failure to keep the body in a clean, healthy state; for overwork and intemperance in eating, in drinking, and in proper care of the body; for the wrong use of his faculties, which cause worry and fear that tear down natural and spiritual resistance to sickness; for certain conditions that pass on from one generation to another; and for failure to appropriate the benefits for which Jesus died so that he can be healed and delivered from satanic powers. Sins of all kinds, rebellion, and misuse of the tongue, hardness of heart, fleshly lusts, pride, unbelief, and many other personal acts on the part of men have caused them to break the laws of God and give the agents of sin, sickness, and death the opportunity to bring about sickness in their lives. This vulnerability does not mean that demons always take advantage at once, for sometimes it is to their advantage not to use their powers to bring sickness upon the law-breakers. But eventually those who sow will have to reap.*

We can see then that whatever we permit into our lives, whether through commission or omission, we reap the results. It is vitally important for us to carry through with what we believe from God's word and reap God's best. If we know what is good, but fail to carry on to obedience, we could reap sins results and end up attaching ourselves to demons and their dark deeds.

There are examples of this.

Examples

A mountain: Jesus told His disciples that if they would believe and not doubt they would see results.[4] Their faith, obviously, would be based upon what they believed. If their belief was faulty they would not realize the desired

---

[4] Matthew 21:21 Jesus replied, "I tell you the truth, if you have faith and do not doubt, not only can you do what was done to the fig tree, but also you can say to this mountain, 'Go, throw yourself into the sea,' and it will be done. 22 If you believe, you will receive whatever you ask for in prayer."

results of what they asked for or commanded in spiritual realms.

It must be noted here, that before the disciples could see the mountain cast into the sea in the natural realm they first must believe that it was possible based upon spiritual truths from God's word and will.

Wisdom: James the Apostle tells us that our request of God most be founded upon solid belief and no doubts.[5] This belief must refrain from any double-mindedness. Double-mindedness, as mentioned before with commission, must remain solidly on what God has said and promised; there is no room for duplicity.

---

[5] James 1:6 But when he asks, he must believe and not doubt, because he who doubts is like a wave of the sea, blown and tossed by the wind. 7 That man should not think he will receive anything from the Lord; 8 he is a double-minded man, unstable in all he does.

Also, wisdom will not be given to the person who is double-minded and unstable[6]. Those people who are unstable and lacking control claim some truths but will compromise for many different reasons which often nullifies faith. I will discuss this in a later chapter.

Double-mindedness and doubt cause us to disqualify ourselves from God's best and we usually end up expecting the negative. Faith can't and won't function properly and double-mindedness makes us see God as a fickle being.

Obedience: [7] Disobedience puts a person in the realm of Satan, who was

---

[6] FICKLE : VACILLATING;   also   : lacking effective emotional control

[7] Romans 2:6 God "will give to each person according to what he has done." 7 To those who by persistence in doing good seek glory, honor and immortality, he will give eternal life. 8 But for those who are self-seeking and who reject the truth and follow evil, there will be wrath and anger.

the first rebel. Rebellion is the deliberate choice to disregard God's will. Rebellion usually comes as a result of a person seeking self-gratification and disregarding the consequence. Once we know this truth it is so very important that we carry through with persistent action and proper choices.

Our persistence must totally deny anything that is contrary to God's will and word. We must have an attitude that demands holiness, righteousness, and purity. We must demand that we refuse evil in any form, no matter how subtle or benign it may appear.

I have found that most Christians give into weaknesses, faults, and anti-God associations because they refuse to see that there must be a disconnect from the world and all its trappings of darkness. These trappings take on many forms and usually are very subtle.

A good rule to follow would be a rule that would require us to walk in any truth that God makes known to us. Even if those truths go against some long held ideas, beliefs, celebrations, or practices.

We can see then, that our belief system makes all the difference on how we walk out our Christianity. If we fail to put the proper importance to God's word and the efficacy inherent in it, we will fail to realize many other things that can make us victorious and accomplish much for the Lord.

Everything we believe or fail to believe, or mix with any falsehoods of darkness, makes up our total belief system. That belief system drives our heart (soul or center) and causes us to accept or deny the promises of God.[8]

Our beliefs must not have any room for careless words or the acceptance of anything that is not of God or that comes from the world. If we do not guard what we believe we may accept things that can destroy our faith and cause us to question God's power and promises.

---

[8] Matt 12:33 "Make a tree good and its fruit will be good, or make a tree bad and its fruit will be bad, for a tree is recognized by its fruit. 34 You brood of vipers, how can you who are evil say anything good? For out of the overflow of the heart the mouth speaks. 35 The good man brings good things out of the good stored up in him, and the evil man brings evil things out of the evil stored up in him. 36 But I tell you that men will have to give account on the day of judgment for every careless word they have spoken. 37 For by your words you will be acquitted, and by your words you will be condemned."

2

Ignorance

Someone once said that ignorance is bliss. I'm not sure if ignorance is bliss, but I do know that ignorance can be deadly.

In the Old Testament God addressed the question of ignorance and graphically commanded what must be done. God's stance against sins committed in ignorance and those committed willfully was basically the same. He did make a way when someone sinned in ignorance to be forgiven and reconciled, but did not diminish the wickedness of the sin. Sin separates humans from God and ignorance is no excuse once a person is informed of it.

Numbers 15:27 And if any soul sin through ignorance, then he shall bring a she goat of the first year for a sin offering.28 And the priest shall make an atonement for the soul that sinneth ignorantly, when he sinneth by ignorance before the Lord, to make an atonement for him; and it shall be forgiven him. 29 Ye shall have one law for him that sinneth through ignorance, both for him that is born among the children of Israel, and for the stranger that sojourneth among them. 30 But the soul that doeth ought presumptuously, whether he be

born in the land, or a stranger, the same reproacheth the Lord; and that soul shall be cut off from among his people. 31 Because he hath despised the word of the Lord, and hath broken his commandment, that soul shall utterly be cut off; his iniquity shall be upon him. KJV

Someone once said, *I guess God still blesses us in our ignorance.* I'm not sure that is correct. If God sees sins committed in ignorance and those committed in rebellion as the same, then He can't bless those who sin.

Now I know what someone will say, *What about the verse that states, "He lets the rain fall on the just as well as the unjust?"* Trying to use that verse to prove that ignorance is an excuse to sin is ridiculous at best. Yes, God does let the rain fall on the just and the unjust, but once either is given the truth they are no longer ignorant.

Once a person is given the truth and they acknowledge it they then stand under the law which either condemns or acquits the sinner. This reality is brought out very well in Numbers 15: 30 **But the soul that doeth ought presumptuously, whether he be born in the land, or a stranger, the same reproacheth the Lord; and that soul shall be cut off from among his people. 31 <u>Because he hath despised the word of the Lord, and hath broken his commandment,</u> that soul shall utterly be cut off; his iniquity shall be upon him. KJV** (underline added)

When a person comes to the Lord and claims to be a son or daughter of God, through Jesus, they then stand in a different spiritual position then they did before.

Ephesians 4:17 So I tell you this, and insist on it in the Lord, that you must no longer live as the Gentiles do, in the futility (ignorance) of their thinking. 18 They are darkened in their understanding and separated from the life of God because of the ignorance that is in them due to the hardening of their hearts.

Their new spiritual position is to be walking in the life of God. In that life there is freedom, joy, peace, healing, needs being met, and provision provided for. If we continue to live out those things we know are wrong we are no longer in ignorance, but only rebellion. That rebellion then will nullify the blessings that God would desire for us.

Jesus spoke of the willful ignorance that we can fall prey to when He came to Jerusalem. Matthew 23:37 *"O Jerusalem, Jerusalem, you who kill the prophets and stone those sent to you, how often I have longed to gather your children together, as a hen gathers her chicks under her wings, but you were not willing. 38 Look, your house is left to you desolate. 39 For I tell you, you will not see me again until you say, 'Blessed is he who comes in the name of the Lord.'"*

The *"but you were not willing"* statement was spoken to a nation and city that refused the truth even when it was standing in their presence. God wanted to give greater blessing to His people and special city, but they were trying to live in two realms. One realm was the realm of legalism and the other was the realm of false repentance. Legalism demanded the adherence to many manmade laws while false repentance approached God without obedience.

You see, we think that God will bless us in our ignorance, all the while knowing truth, but continuing in our disobedience. God wants to bless, but He can't release the best because we try to live in two realms. Ignorance doesn't even play a role as we claim to be Christians and have been given the truth.

We all too often miss God's blessings because we try to live our Christianity in the two realms mentioned above. We unwittingly go along with things that have to do with spiritual darkness, or border on spiritual darkness, all the while seeking blessings from God but failing to see much of it being materialized in our life.

I believe we don't see all that God has for us because we permit false gods to live among us. I don't necessarily believe we willfully worship or accept false gods, but I do believe we go along with many things that false gods are attached to or originated with false gods and the things of spiritual darkness.

It must be understood that demons attach themselves to anything that has to do with false worship, idols, and gods or goddess in any form. It is those demons that cause much sickness and abnormalities in body, soul, and spirit. Often people will not realize freedom until they rid themselves of the object, spiritual power or ungodly association, and then repent and turn to God.

God asks the question "**What communion hath light with**

darkness?" We must know how to answer the question and then follow through with proper and decisive action.

3

The gods Among Us

It is sad that so many people do not realize the benefits of blessing because they align themselves with forces of darkness and end up only reaping the results of curse.

If I would claim that many Christians worship false gods, I'm sure I would have an argument on my hands. If I would claim that many Christians willfully rebel against God, I would probably have less of an argument. If I would claim that we tend to pick and choose which truths of God's word we accept and then live, I'm sure I would not have much of an argument as most of us know that we tend to do this. But, as God's children, shouldn't we walk in the truths that we are informed of? I say yes we should, and must, for our own well-being!

I'm afraid that we miss out on many of the blessings that God wants to bring us because we have associations with false gods that are among us.

I know that that statement is drastic and shocking. I know that we would want to argue the point and probably use the ignorance card to make our point. But, before you throw this book away, please give me more time and pages to help you understand where I'm coming from.

The gods among us

I want to make something very clear in this section. When I talk about the gods among us, I am putting anything that is contrary to God's will and biblically stated ways in the same category. I have come to realize that humans align themselves with either God's power or the powers of darkness. The powers of darkness obviously are in Satan's realm and he is the author of anything that pulls mankind away from biblical truth and God's commands.

If I would ask you, *"Do you check out a horoscope? What is your Zodiac sign? Do* you believe in luck? Do you check out astrology? What about the rabbit's foot or the horse shoe, do you think they help in any way? Do you believe Jesus is the only way to God the Father or is there another way? Do you believe in numerology or ever use the Ouija board?"

Let's look at just one example of permitting false gods or the belief in those things that are against God's word. Let's take astrology;

After the warning against adding anything to God's Word in Deuteronomy 4:2, the Lord adds this: ***"And take heed, lest you lift your eyes to heaven, and when you see the sun, the moon, and the stars, all the host of heaven, you feel driven to worship them and serve them, which the Lord your God has given to all the peoples under the***

whole heaven as a heritage (4:19)." The word translated "serve" in that verse means "to be subject to." (You make yourself subject to the stars when you follow them or believe in them or seek them for guidance.)

God expressly forbids astrology, which is a form of interpreting omens, and places it in the same category as witchcraft and child sacrifice (Deuteronomy 18:10-14). He does not want us to place ourselves in spiritual and moral subjection to the stars and planets, but to Scripture alone. Anyone who claims to be a Christian but also studies his horoscope is denying the authority of God's Word, and following a false and spiritually deadly authority — that of Satan himself.

God specifically identified astrologers as among those who will experience the fire of His judgment: ***You are wearied in the multitude of your counsels; let now the astrologers, the stargazers, and the monthly prognosticators stand up and save you from what shall come upon you. Behold, they shall be as stubble, the fire shall burn them; they shall not deliver themselves from the power of the flame; it shall not be a coal to be warmed by, nor a fire to sit before!*** (Isaiah 47:13-14)

Virtually every pagan religion, both ancient and modern (including Buddhism and Hinduism today) involves some form of astrology using the Zodiac.

I believe many people have associations with false gods by giving false gods an innocent, but permissible right into their lives. An example would be the daily checking of horoscopes.

Now, before I go on, please bear with me, and have an open, but prayerful heart and mind.

Most Christians celebrate Easter. This holiday celebrates Jesus' resurrection. Easter is the name of a false goddess and most of the Easter celebration is directly associated with this false goddess. Even its name comes from the goddess Astrate.

God tells us in Exodus 23:*13* ***"Be careful to do everything I have said to you. Do not invoke the names of other gods; do not let them be heard on your lips."*** Easter has a false goddess name, and the eggs, bunnies, forty days of fasting, sunrise services, and the like all come from this false god. I address this false goddess in my book *Easter – Not What You Think.*

When a person celebrates the Resurrection and uses the name Easter, permits the eggs, bunnies and the pagan trappings of Easter, a person is giving a false goddess credence, whether they believe it or not. God forbids it even in ignorance! I believe we should celebrate the Resurrection, but we must not call it Easter.

Luck

God tells us that our time on this earth should be directed by Him. He speaks to us in His word, Holy Scripture, and informs us that if we will acknowledge Him and His ways He will direct our steps. ***"The steps of a good man are ordered by the Lord: and he*** *delighteth in his way. Though he fall, he shall not be utterly cast down: for the Lord upholdeth him with his hand."* Psalms 37:23-24 KJV.

We can see that God gives no room for luck or happenstance, either a person lets God direct his steps or he doesn't. If he doesn't then he is at the mercy of the world, weather, and the corrupted wisdom of man.

Luck is not an inexplicable force that cannot be understood, explained, or accounted for.

It is certainly true that there are many things that are not understood in life, but luck is not one of them. The superstitious beliefs that are taught about a "luck-force" existing beyond human knowledge and comprehension add up to nothing more than groundless, off-beat speculation. The natural-minded, irrational man has imagined the existence of a force called luck, and then says, "It can't be explained." So the non-existent, but popular imagined force of luck has developed into a catchall explanation for good and evil. But, the only forthright and truthful explanation for the forces of good and evil are clearly spelled out in God's Word. There are no other spiritual forces affecting our lives, beyond those that are thoroughly explained by God's Word.

Luck is not an innocent, harmless, crutch-word that can be used without any real impact or consequences. It is not a harmless activity to contradict God and the truth of His Word. God promises in His Word that He is the legitimate and genuine bestower of blessings and benefits, and that true prosperity comes by Him alone.

Using the so-called lucky items, such as the rabbit's foot, horse shoes, lucky stars, astrology, numerology, and the horoscope is seeking direction and protection outside of God.

When a Christian uses the above mentioned items or has a luck directed attitude they are trying to seek direction from sources other than God. When the Christian does this he/she is opening themselves up to the influences of demons and Satan. In this duplicitous state God cannot bless or give guidance because He refuses to allow darkness and light to co-mingle.

Mediums

It always amazes me when I hear of someone consulting a medium, fortune teller, or psychic. I know of Christians that do this and can't understand that what they are doing is in direct rebellion to God and His word. *'"Do not turn to mediums or seek out spiritists, for you will be defiled by them. I am the Lord your God.* Leviticus 19:31. Being defiled by this association can cause sickness and poverty in many forms.

The people who seek mediums, fortune tellers, or psychics are placing themselves under the demon that controls those individuals. The medium may deny any association with demons, but in their ignorance they are being controlled never-the-less.

I'm sure you have seen the well-known T.V. mediums and seers who claim to speak to the dead or are being led by the dead. Many of these misguided individuals even believe they are being led by God. They sound nice, comforting, and convincing, but believe me, they are being fooled and defiled, along with those who seek out their services.

When Christians seek out any guidance, other than Godly guidance, they are opening themselves up to doctrines of demons.

Now the Spirit speaketh expressly, that in the latter times some shall depart from the faith, giving heed to seducing spirits, and doctrines of devils; Speaking lies in hypocrisy; having their conscience seared with a hot iron; 1 Timothy 4:1-2 KJV

Ouija board[9]

The Ouija board has been used, or maybe I should say, played with by many people throughout the world. This supposedly innocent game played with one, two or more people has brought laughs and giggles to unsuspecting seekers.

It too has its foundation in the realm of demons and was used as a means of ostensibly contacting the dead and the spirit-world.

---

[9] Chao Wei-pang. 1942. "The origin and Growth of the Fu Chi", Folklore Studies 1:9–27 "One of the first mentions of the automatic writing method used in the Ouija board is found in China around 1100 AD, in historical documents of the Song Dynasty. The method was known as "planchette writing". The use of planchette writing as a means of ostensibly contacting the dead and the spirit-world continued, and, albeit under special rituals and supervisions, was a central practice of the Quanzhen School, until it was forbidden by the Qing Dynasty.[9] Several entire scriptures of the Daozang are supposedly works of automatic planchette writing. Similar methods of mediumistic spirit writing have been widely practiced in ancient India, Greece, Rome, and medieval Europe."

I personally know of relatives and friends who have constantly used the Ouija board to seek guidance for their lives.

I know of a woman and her daughter who used the Ouija board often and even saw a form of another being in their mirror which they called their spiritual guide. This woman and her daughter had constant sicknesses and in the mother's case died young. Both of these woman confessed that they were Christian, but they never seemed to be free from strange sickness or mental confusion.

Idols we permit

We can permit, often in ignorance, false gods to live among us in the form of figurines. You know the type; the fat little Buddha that is bought on a trip someplace, the slim Indian god that is oh so cute, the sign of the Zodiac above the door or hanging on the wall, the horse shoe on the door, the lucky charm, or the pretty silver Egyptian Ankh that is worn around one's neck[10].

All of the above mentioned items have to do with false gods and have their origin in the powers of darkness. These items are in direct conflict with Christian principles and a proper walk with God. They represent a form of belief or trust in the god or goddess they represent, either overtly or covertly. And when found within one's home gives permission for demons to come in. They are in direct conflict with God's command not to have them in one's home or on one's person.

---

[10] ☥ The ankh appears frequently in Egyptian tomb paintings and other art, often at the fingertips of a god or goddess in images that represent the deities of the afterlife conferring the gift of life on the dead person's mummy.

Through the above mentioned associations the unsuspecting individuals open themselves up to the curses that come from their possession and attachment.

I have often ministered to families who had problems with sickness, poverty, and some sort of mental confusion, but could not find freedom. While ministering to these families I have found they owned and displayed a figurine of Buddha, Indian god, or other such statue. After sharing with these families the dangers of possessing a representation of a false god they destroyed the item and almost instantly found freedom and release.

The above mentioned families were Christian confessing families and did not understand the dangers that are associated with false gods. They, like many, had the items in ignorance or saw them as cute little figurines. This should be a good lesson to us all!

4

Total Freedom Demands Oneness

As I have discussed earlier, we must walk out our life with God in a *one-realm-reality.* What I mean by a *one-realm-reality* is that we must not permit anything into our life that has to do with the realm of Satan, demons, or false religions and their gods.

I have met Christians who have told me many frustrating stories of not realizing freedom, but claim to love the Lord, follow His instructions, and walk the best way they know how.

Before we go further, we need to understand a very foundational truth. Always remember, God is not the problem, His word is always correct, and His ways to walk with Him are set in spiritual cement. God does not vary in His love, fairness, and commands. He means what He says and requires our utmost obedience and love.

One of the founding realities of a proper walk with God is a zeroing in on seeking Him above all else. ***But seek first his kingdom and his righteousness, and all these things***

will be given to you as well. Matthew 6:33-34

The seeking first principle must deny anything, let me repeat, anything, that denies God, refuses to trust Him, or comes from the darker elements of life and the wrong spirit realm. Any of those things mentioned in the previous chapter are of the wrong spiritual realm.

We tie God's hands when we permit anything of Satan, those things of spiritual dark nature, or out-right rebellion to His word and commands.

If we fail to obey God and find sickness, confusion, or lack in our life we should pretty well know that we have failed to obey God or have let something into our lives that is not of God. However, He is such a gentleman and will not force us to give up those things we demand to deem more important than Him. It is our choice!

Often I have ministered to people who have had in their homes the items mentioned in chapter three, but could not be healed, set free, or find rest until they repented and discarded the items.

I have ministered to many people who seemingly have done all the proper spiritual things, according to scripture, but still lack healing or freedom.

After careful and personal research I found that the one thing that made the difference in their freedom was their association with items, beliefs or actions that were contrary to God and His will and ways.

Because these individuals confessed to know the truth, but failed to act upon those truths they felt guilty and therefore disqualified themselves from receiving God's best. This disqualification came by way of doubt, double mindedness, and fear.

God is a jealous[11] being. God is not a jealous being as we are, but a jealous being that will not permit the enemy of our souls to co-mingle with us. His jealousy is a protective form of jealousy.

"You shall not make for yourself an idol in the form of anything in heaven above or on the earth beneath or in the waters below. 5 You shall not bow down to them or worship them; for I, the Lord your God, am a jealous God, punishing the children for the sin of the fathers to the third and fourth generation of those who hate me, 6 but showing love to a thousand [generations] of those who love me and keep my commandments. Exodus 20:4

---

[11] Jealous - 1 : demanding complete devotion, 2 : suspicious of a rival or of one believed to enjoy an advantage, 3 : VIGILANT

God is a being who will not share His love for His children with powers of darkness, He also will not force His children to walk with Him. Their desire must come from free-will, but they must understand that with free-will comes responsibility.

If a Christian permits the items and celebrations mentioned above, God will step back and let them witness, realize, and benefit from their association with darkness. God will still love the child, but they will not realize the full benefits as one of His children. They must break off any association with idols, false gods, or the practices that are contrary to God's will and ways.

(Note: When it states in Exodus 20: 5 that *am a jealous God, punishing the children for the sin of the fathers to*

46

the third and fourth generation of those who hate me...it must understood that this is the only place in scripture that states that God brings a curse upon someone. That curse would only be brought upon the third and fourth generations of idol worshippers and those in that category who hate Him. It has no other application to any other individual or their descendants. And of course it must be understood that no Christian would fall into that category, period. The Christian has freedom from the power of any curse because Jesus became a curse for us![12])

---

[12] Gal 3:13-14Christ has redeemed us from the curse of the law, having become a curse for us (for it is written, "Cursed is everyone who hangs on a tree"), 14 that the blessing of Abraham might come upon the Gentiles in Christ Jesus, that we might receive the promise of the Spirit through faith. NKJV

Knowledge brings freedom

My people are destroyed for lack of knowledge: because thou hast rejected knowledge, I will also reject thee,
Hosea 4:66 KJV.

When we realize truth we have responsibility for that truth. We can't say we don't have the knowledge to be free and capable of realizing God's best once we know the truth. It is the very truth and understanding that God wants His children to be free from any association with demons, Satan, and the powers of darkness that separates true believers from those who will not submit to truth. If we confess Jesus and profess to believe God's word, we then are responsible to walk in all aspects of His word.

We cannot associate ourselves with the Zodiac, the name Easter (this is a false goddess), Astrology, Numerology,

Buddha, Rabbit's Foot, Krishna, Charms, Ouija board, Palm readers, daily Horoscope, or Mediums and walk in the fullness of God and the freedom He desires for His children. There are consequences with those associations and it is always bad. Those associations bring sickness, infirmity, loss, poverty, and death in all forms.

Repentance is required!

Repent! Turn away from all your offenses; then sin will not be your downfall. 31 Rid yourselves of all the offenses you have committed, and get a new heart and a new spirit. Why will you die, O house of Israel? 32 For I take no pleasure in the death of anyone, declares the Sovereign Lord. Repent and live! Ezekiel 18:30-32.

Once we accept the truth and repent God promises to restore and heal. What we do with the truth given in this book can be a liberating reality or it can become a curse to us.

Scripture informs us that a curse cannot come to those who walk with God, but if we refuse God and His word a curse could come to us. The willful act of denying truth would be a reason for a curse to come.

Like a fluttering sparrow or a darting swallow, an undeserved curse does not come to rest. Proverbs 26:2

The curse would be self-imposed because one would refuse the truth. God would not bring the curse, but the refusal of God's word would give Satan and his demons permission to come into one's life and bring chaos **_(this does not necessarily mean demon possession, but rather demon harassment)_**.

What will you do with this truth?

5

The power of blessing

Before we realize the power of blessing I think it is most important for us to understand curse.

Curse is the word καταράομαι (kataraomai = kat-ar-ah'-om-ahee) in Greek, meaning to execrate or ex-out of sacred: to denounce as evil or detestable.

Also the definition of cursing means *a calling on God or the gods to send evil or injury down on some person or thing.*

In other words when we think of curse or cursing we must think in the terms of scripture and how cursing comes about. Cursing is speaking a negative pronouncement upon oneself, others, and accepting the consequence of the negative implied.

When God would curse a nation or individual He was execrating them from the sacred and denouncing their actions and intentions as detestable and they would not receive any good from Him.

Also when an individual is pronouncing a curse upon himself or pronouncing anything other than what God would pronounce upon him he is accepting something that God does not proclaim nor sanction about him.

Also, when we think of someone under a curse this is most often someone who is constantly having problems that are common in their families. It usually is a trait, ongoing addiction, personality occurrences, and/or other learned life style that is detrimental to them. These people will often blame or think they need to forgive their ancestry for the curse that was on them. In all actuality those things are not a curse in the true sense of its meaning, but nevertheless are seen as something they had no control over.

If someone would argue the case for God cursing the children to the third or fourth generation as seen in Exodus

20:5[13], one must understand the nature of this one time and special curse. First, it would be pronounced upon the Hebrew people who were idolaters, who hated God and refused His sovereignty. This curse was not toward anyone other than those specific individuals or nation.

As far as God bringing a curse to families in general, this is not found in scripture. In most cases that God speaks of curses it is in reference to a people (usually, the Hebrews) who would not obey and then they would be a detriment to the peoples and societies they were in. The curse was not a pronouncement from God but a fact of the peoples anti God lifestyle and stubbornness of heart. And,

---

[13] Exodus 20:5, Thou shalt not bow down thyself to them, nor serve them: for I the thy God am a jealous, visiting the iniquity of the fathers upon the children unto the third and fourth generation of them that hate me;

it was their actions and continued lifestyle that caused their own harm.

All too often what we call a curse on our lives or on someone else's life is the observed lifestyles that fall short of a Godly lifestyle in general, or a learned family trait that is contrary to a holy life.

We must never forget a very simple and exact truth; Jesus became a curse for us on the cross. Every person who comes to Jesus in simple faith is free from any curse, period. There is no demon, no ancestor's action or lifestyle that can bring a curse through the shed blood of our savior. Jesus has set us free from the curse of the law or any other curse and has made possible for the blessings of Abraham to come to us. The

Christian is a recipient of blessing and not curse[14].

To repeat myself, If there seems to be an ongoing problem with a Christian it is not a curse, but could be a learned family trait, a recommitted sin, or a refusal to turn from things that are detrimental to a Godly life.

Blessing

Blessing has an innate power. It is an ability that God gives and has the creative power that comes directly from Him to those who choose to function as He would.[15] [16]

---

[14]Gal 3:13-14 Christ has redeemed us from the curse of the law, having become a curse for us (for it is written, "Cursed is everyone who hangs on a tree"), 14 that the blessing of Abraham might come upon the Gentiles in Christ Jesus, that we might receive the promise of the Spirit through faith. NKJV
[15] Ephesians 1:3, Blessed be the God and Father of our Lord Jesus Christ, who has blessed us with all spiritual blessings in heavenly places in Christ:4, According as he has chosen us in him before the foundation of the world, that we should be holy and without blame before him in love:5, Having predestinated us to the adoption of children by Jesus Christ to himself, according to the good pleasure of

Scripture tells us *to bless those who persecute you; bless and do not curse.*[17] We have the creative ability as God's children to not respond as the world responds but to make the choice to speak well of those who either curse us (speak evil of or treat us badly) or persecute us.

Blessing in reference to the above verse means to *speak well of, invoke a benediction, or praise.* In other words the Christian is to be a person who is always looking for ways to speak well of

---

his will, 6, To the praise of the glory of his grace, wherein he has made us accepted in the beloved. 7, In whom we have redemption through his blood, the forgiveness of sins, according to the riches of his grace;8, Wherein he has abounded toward us in all wisdom and prudence; 9, Having made known to us the mystery of his will, according to his good pleasure which he has purposed in himself: 10, That in the dispensation of the fullness of times he might gather together in one all things in Christ, both which are in heaven, and which are on earth; even in him:11, In whom also we have obtained an inheritance, being predestinated according to the purpose of him who works all things after the counsel of his own will:12, That we should be to the praise of his glory, who first trusted in Christ.

[16]1 Peter 3: 9, Not rendering evil for evil, or railing for railing: but contrariwise blessing; knowing that you are thereunto called, that you should inherit a blessing.

[17] Romans 12:14, Bless them that persecute you; bless, and curse not.

someone, or to praise them, or ask God to prosper or bring good to them.

1 Peter 3:8 and 9, Finally, be ye all likeminded, compassionate, loving as brethren, tenderhearted, humble minded; not rendering evil for evil, or reviling for reviling; but contrariwise blessing; for hereunto were ye called, that ye should inherit a blessing.

The above verses tell us that blessing's power has the ability to create an atmosphere of good. It is compassionate, loving, tenderhearted, humble, and may I add, understanding.

We can realize from 1 Peter 3:8-9 that blessing comes from a heartfelt understanding on the part of the one who is blessing. It is a choice one makes in spite of any circumstance or happenings at the moment. It comes from knowledge that God blesses us even when we don't deserve it. It crosses over any and all barriers and strikes to the heart in love. It denies hate, discord, and prejudices. It simply puts face to the unseen personality of love.

No judgment

To bless, one must not make a negative judgment as to the people being blessed or of oneself. It may understand the weaknesses and sin that others may have, but it does not require conformity, repentance or submission before the blessing may come. It just blesses and leaves the judgment up to God.

God is the one who makes judgments and His knowledge is infinite. He can require change, repentance, or surrender before He brings blessings but it is His divine choice whether to do so or not.

Jesus' teaching in Matthew 5:3-12 gives us a very good look as to the blessing and the subject of judgment.

(verse 3, Matthew 5) <u>"Blessed are the poor in spirit"</u>

A. Jesus spoke and demonstrated that abasement was the way to achievement. (die to live, give away to receive, and be humble to be exalted)
   1. To gain heaven you must be humble in your opinion of yourself, remembering that you are a sinner saved by God's favor and not your abilities.
   2. Jesus wants us to see ourselves as we really are - without hope if it were not for Him.
B. We must confess our weaknesses and the reality of His favor.
   1. Never forget the fact of your human state without Jesus.
C. If we will learn the humbleness of poverty, we will see the kingdom of heaven.
   1. Never forget from where you came.

(verse 4, Matthew 5) <u>"Blessed are those who mourn"</u>

D. We must learn to mourn over sin.
   1. Sin in our lives and in the lives of others…friends, relatives, and associates…home, state, country, and world.

2. This mourning over sin should drive us to our knees at the slightest sin in others and ourselves.

E. Our mourning over sin must come from the thought that sin grieves God and not that I just was caught.

    1. When is the last time you cried over sin?

F. If we will mourn over sin, then we will be blessed and comforted and great things will come our way. *Isai 61:2 (KJS) To proclaim the acceptable year of the LORD, and the day of vengeance of our God; to comfort all that mourn; 3 To appoint unto them that mourn in Zion, to give unto them beauty for ashes, the oil of joy for mourning, the garment of praise for the spirit of heaviness; that they might be called trees of righteousness, the planting of the LORD, that he might be glorified.*

    1. A crown of beauty: (an embellishment or a gleam or ornament or something that stands out)

        a. He will show you off as an example of His heart toward forgiveness from sin.

    2. The oil of gladness: (oil represents the Holy Spirit and gladness means joy) - He will bestow on you the joy of the Holy Spirit.

        a. This mourning over sin is much different from the heaviness of human mourning over issues that do not matter...this mourning goes to the very heart of who you are and what you believe and then brings inner peace and deep happiness of the Spirit of God.

3. The garment of praise: (this praise comes from a heart that is really free because of forgiveness)
   a. It will not be a task to praise God or loudly sing forth the greatness and beauty of God.
   b. It will be a part of your everyday life.
   c. It will not have to be worked up.
4. All this is because God wants to display His splendor in you.

(verse 5, Matthew 5) <u>"Blessed are the meek"</u> (they will inherit the earth)

meek adj. 1. Showing patience and humility; gentle. 2. Easily imposed on; submissive. --meek"ly adv.
   A. The meekness Jesus teaches us is not a weak and shy personality; it is composure through and in all situations that depicts submission to and a trust in God.
      1. This meekness does not defend itself nor flaunt its power, goods, or abilities; it totally trusts God.
      2. The church submits to God's word, God's rod, and God's direction...this depicts meekness.
   B. Jesus wants us to be patient in the reception of injuries, not surrendering our rights to evil, but only to God, not being cowardice.
      1. It is the opposite of sudden anger or malice or long-harbored vengeance.
      2. Meekness maintains the attitude that vengeance is God's.

C. Meekness produces peace. It comes from a heart too great to be moved by little insults.
   1. The person who is not trying to learn meekness is easily ruffled...he can be easily troubled and fall prey to the person who desires to bother him.
D. The meek person will inherit the earth.
   1. "To inherit the earth" was a Hebraic term meaning to possess the land of Canaan. *Psal 37:7 (NIV) Be still before the LORD and wait patiently for him; do not fret when men succeed in their ways, when they carry out their wicked schemes. 8 Refrain from anger and turn from wrath; do not fret--it leads only to evil. 9 For evil men will be cut off, but those who hope in the LORD will inherit the land. 10 A little while, and the wicked will be no more; though you look for them, they will not be found. 11 But the meek will inherit the land and enjoy great peace.*
      a. This would only come if Israel would "meekly" receive God's direction and ways.
      b. Only through meekness can earthly things be safe under God's protection. *1Tim 4:8 (NIV) For physical training is of some value, but godliness has value for all things, holding promise for both the present life and the life to come.*

(verse 6, Matthew 5) <u>"Blessed are those who hunger and thrust for righteousness"</u> (they will be filled)

A. You must hunger for spiritual food or, like with the lack of natural food, you will perish.
   1. Desire righteousness to the point of pain (pain of denying self and the desires of the flesh, which can bring spiritual death), and you "will be filled!"
   2. Only through a deep inner craving for God and His ways can there be true fulfillment.
      a. Natural hunger can make a person do anything to be fed...we must be like a starving person for righteousness.
      b. Hunger is not satisfied with a little taste, it wants "all." (Do you want all there is of righteousness in Christ?)
      c. If you will be as diligent to seek God and righteousness as you are to eat food, you will be filled and satisfied in your spirit.
      d. Satisfaction cannot be found in two camps - camp of the Lord and the camp of the world...it is only found in the camp of God.

(verse 7, Matthew 5)   "Blessed are the merciful" (They will receive mercy)
   A. Mercy is the nature of God. *Deut 4:31 (NIV) For the LORD your God is a merciful God; he will not abandon or destroy you or forget the covenant with your forefathers, which he confirmed to them by oath.*
      1. Jesus tells us to be God like by showing mercy.

a. Every circumstance in Jesus' dealing with mankind was/is merciful...from the women caught in adultery to the demon possessed man.
b. Although sin creates the negative circumstances of life, mercy must be the dictating and motivating tool used to bring redemption and reconciliation to others.
c. Mercy remembers from where you came and how God forgave you.
d. Mercy goes out of its way to show compassion and give help.
e. Mercy never sees the opening to take the advantage, but gives the advantage to the other person who needs it more.

B. Mercy attracts holiness and repels condemnation.

(verse 8, Matthew 5)   "Blessed are the pure in heart...they will see God."

A. "Pure" means, to "clean out" in Greek= katharos, in English=catharsis or cauterize. It is a cleaning out by force or drawing out.
1. Only by a complete cleaning of our heart can we really see God.
2. We must purge everything that would taint us and keep us from seeing God face to face in spirit. *1 Cor 5:6 Your boasting is not good. Don't you know that a little yeast works through the whole batch of dough? 7 Get rid of the old yeast that you may be a new batch without yeast — as you really*

are. For Christ, our Passover lamb, has been sacrificed. NIV

    a. The cleansing agent of the word can purge you, if you will let it. *Eph 5:25 Husbands, love your wives, just as Christ loved the church and gave himself up for her 26 to make her holy, cleansing her by the washing with water through the word, 27 and to present her to himself as a radiant church, without stain or wrinkle or any other blemish, but holy and blameless. NIV*

    b. The word shows you the sickness, the sin, and the strengths.

        (1.) You do have strengths, therefore, purge the sin and you will realize strengths.

  3. Your heart must be as pure as love and untainted by a conscience of sin. *1 Tim 1:5 The goal of this command is love, which comes from a pure heart and a good conscience and a sincere faith. NIV*

    a. We must practice love...(really overlooking wrong done to self, seeking the best for others and going the extra mile to show support.)

B. The pure in heart are the only ones capable of seeing God.

  1. It would be painful and produce much shame and condemnation for the impure of heart.

  2. The pure in heart are not satisfied with anything less than to see God.

a. Seeing God in spirit and recognizing Him at work in your life is seeing God. What a blessing it is to see God and have His approval in heart.

(verse 9, Matthew 5)   "Blessed are the peacemakers...the sons of God"
   A. A peacemaker, above all else, must know Jesus who is the Prince of Peace!
      1. Peacemakers know Jesus by faith, experience and His presence daily.
         A. Faith: The peacemaker believes in the suffering, death, and resurrection of Christ on his behalf.
         b. Experience: The peacemaker knows the peace that passes understanding because he knows it from his own born-again experience.
         c. Presence: The peacemaker communes with Christ daily and receives direction from God in everything.
   B. The peacemaker goes out of his way to end arguments, right wrongs, reconcile differences, and calm the storm of negative emotion.
   C. A peacemaker does not delight in wrong done to anyone, even enemies.
      1. They always forgive and forget.
      2. They yield their mind to the Holy Spirit. *Rom 8:5 Those who live according to the sinful nature have their minds set on what that nature desires; but those who live in accordance with the Spirit have their minds set on what the Spirit desires. NIV*

a. Inner peace is a mark of a peacemaker.
  (1.)   Peace will elude a person who is always finding fault, accusing, and speaking negative.
  (2.)   If peace be your aim, peace will you gain!

(verse 10-12, Matthew 5)   "Blessed are you when persecuted…yours is the kingdom of heaven."
  A. Jesus told us that we would be persecuted because of Him.
    1. *2 Tim 3:12 In fact, everyone who wants to live a godly life in Christ Jesus will be persecuted, NIV*
    2. It is a fact, if you live like you are supposed to in Christ Jesus, persecution will follow you - expect it.
      a. There is a way to avoid persecution:
        (3.)   Keep your mouth shut (pertaining to Jesus).
        (4.)   Do not let anyone know you love the Lord.
        (5.)   Do not lead anyone to Christ.
        (6.)   Do not pray or study the word of God.
        (7.)   Do not speak or act like a Christian.
      b. If you keep your Christianity to yourself and live like the world, you will be accepted and loved by it and those in it. Persecution and temptation go hand in hand. *James 1:2 Consider it pure joy, my brothers, whenever you face trials of*

68

many kinds, 3 because you know that the testing of your faith develops perseverance. NIV

James 1:12 Blessed is the man who perseveres under trial, because when he has stood the test, he will receive the crown of life that God has promised to those who love him. NIV

3. Temptation and persecution make you strong...learn through them.
4. Persecution gives evidence that your home is heaven, because you are separating yourself from the world.

Holiness and righteousness

Jesus' teaching on blessings goes way beyond being on the receiving end of special privileges, gifts, or position in life. He makes the point that to walk in blessing and be a blessing to others one must understand the nature of holiness and righteousness.

Holiness is a topic that is not taught much in the modern church because the modern church has become too entwined with the world. Too often the church has used the ways and means of the world and its systems to further the gospel so much so that it has lost the cleansing agent of separation; thereby not recognizing that blessing is found and realized through separation from the world.

Once we come to an understanding that to be a blessing one must be upright, faithful to God and others. Walking in obedience to truth, purity, and scripture we will find our lives will make a lasting difference. *1 Peter 3:9 not returning evil for evil or reviling for reviling, but on the contrary blessing, knowing that you were called to this, that you may inherit a blessing. NKJV*

We must fully grasp the magnificent power we can possess as God's children.

We must the ability to reach out to others and bless them by our words, actions, and benevolence. In other words we have creative ability given to us from the creator to change lives, repel negative, and promote good. Through these we extend God's blessing to others and reveal His very nature.

Blessing is a choice however! We can't sit back and enjoy the blessings of God and not bless others. The only way it is accomplished is by determined effort to make life better for others and to shine as God's children. Blessing others and being a blessing in society honors God, proves the message of the cross, and repels the darkness in the world.

It isn't enough to talk christianese, our talk must move to the action of blessing which gives expression of our loving Savior who lives in us!

It's a tongue thing!

Death and life are in the power of the tongue,
And those who love it will eat its fruit.
Prov 18:21

When God tells us that death and life are in the tongue He is directing our attention to one of the most powerful realities a child of God must understand. God created through His spoken word, He maintains by the words spoken about creation, and He calls us to be a part of His ongoing blessing to the earth through the power of our tongue with words.

We can bless others by our words, and that blessing opens up spiritual realities that can change a life, either for good or bad. Let's look at how this is done:

James 3:6-12 And the tongue is a fire, a world of iniquity. The tongue is so set among our members that it defiles the whole body, and sets on fire the course of nature; and it is set on fire by hell. 7 For every kind of beast and bird, of reptile and creature of the sea, is tamed and has been tamed by mankind. 8 But no man can tame the tongue. It is an unruly evil, full of deadly poison. 9 With it we bless our God and Father, and with it we curse men, who have been made in the similitude of God. 10 Out of the same mouth proceed blessing and cursing. My brethren, these things ought not to be so. NKJV

Obviously the human tongue is not capable of starting a fire. It does however speak what is in the heart of the one speaking. If the heart and will of the one speaking is established upon righteousness and holiness the tongue will speak accordingly. If the heart of the one speaking does not fear God nor adhere to His will and decrees his tongue will speak evil! Speaking evil is anything contrary to God's word and established on earthly principles instead of Kingdom truths.

But, if we do not control our heart, for out of it comes all kinds of mischief and darkness, we will be cursing instead of blessing.

Since one of the meanings of blessing is "to speak well of", obviously if we are not speaking well of others we are doing the opposite and ending up cursing. By these cursing's we are thinking the worst of people or situations and responding toward them in the negative. When we speak of self, family, or others in the negative, it is as if we are expecting the worst and conduct our actions accordingly.

We can understand this when we examine the words spoken over others, especially children. When parents do not speak loving words over their children but only criticize them, the children usually grow up full of self-loathing and inferiorities. These children see themselves as being under a curse and often think that they cannot receive anything good from God.

It is so very important that we know our heart and examine what we believe and understand from God's word. If we fail to fully grasp the many blessings and what God thinks of us, our heart will never truly know how to bless others. It really does matter what we permit into our heart (our center of understanding).

Luke 6:45 A good man out of the good treasure of his heart brings forth good; and an evil man out of the evil treasure of his heart brings forth evil. For out of the abundance of the heart his mouth speaks. NKJV

True blessings only come from a person whose heart is established upon God, His word, and resting upon the reality of what Jesus did on the cross for him. Through this understanding it is easy for one to bless others and refrain from cursing's that flow from a sick, un-nurtured heart of disappointment, and turmoil.

Jeremiah 17:9 The heart is deceitful above all things, And desperately wicked; Who can know it? 10 I, the Lord, search the heart, I test the mind, Even to give every man according to his ways, According to the fruit of his doings. NKJV

Foundation is key!

To be a blessing insure you have established a foundation which your life stands on and a supporting structure of truth.

First: Are you truly born-again? Have you surrendered all to God?

Second: Have you made your mind up to respond to God's will no matter what?

Third: Do you know that you have a mandate from God to be a blessing in this world?

Fourth: Do understand that you have the power to bless because God has blessed you? Know that God has left nothing out for life and godliness!

Fifth: The only choice you have is the choice to bless and not curse in any form! Our motto must be "I will be a blessing!"

www.ingramcontent.com/pod-product-compliance
Lightning Source LLC
Chambersburg PA
CBHW062017040426
42447CB00010B/2026